Early Childhood Inventory of Multiple Intelligences

Created By

Eileen Palmer, M.Ed. & Katrina Wood, M.Ed.

This book was printed in the United States of America.

To order additional copies of this book, contact:
Xlibris Corporation
1-888-795-4274
www.Xlibris.com
Orders@Xlibris.com

Dedicated to
Morgan, Abigail, Aubrey,
Seth and Andrew Wood.
Without you this inventory
would not have been created.

E.P. & K.W.

Every year teachers are plagued with thoughts of how they will reach students who have problems learning in traditional settings. They encounter students with a variety of abilities that are often "lop-sided'. In other words, children are gifted with a skill or two and yet lack in other areas. For example; teachers encounter students with abilities to create structures with blocks but are unable to verbally explain their work, students able to classify dinosaurs but unable to work together in a group setting, and students who are able to act out elaborate stories yet may not be able to recognize numbers. These are the children that inspired Howard Gardener's theory of Multiple Intelligences.

Multiple Intelligences was introduced by Howard Gardner in 1993 to help teachers understand how to reach students who had trouble learning in traditional settings. He suggests the need to focus attention on the students' intelligences in order for them to achieve success.

This Early Childhood Multiple Intelligence Inventory was adapted from Susan Teele's Inventory and designed to help teachers identify each student's four strongest intelligences so they may develop classroom instruction which targets those intelligences. This tool is a quick assessment for teachers to use in the classroom any time throughout the year and will allow teachers to have the opportunity to develop each student's unique intelligence. It was designed by teachers with teachers in mind.

Key:

1. **Verbal**—the ability to effectively use words orally and in writing

2. **Math/Logical**—the ability to use numbers effectively and reason logically

3. **Visual/Spatial**—the ability to think in pictures and recreate images in their mind or on paper

4. **Bodily/Kinesthetic**—the ability to use the body for self-expression, solve problems, create products, and play games

5. **Music/Rhythmic**—the ability to understand and create music through rhythmic and tonal patterns to express ideas

6. **People-(interpersonal)**—the ability to understand and respond appropriately to others actions, values, moods, and motivations.

7. **Self-(intrapersonal)**—the ability to understand one's own emotions and have a healthy self-esteem

8. **Naturalist**—the ability to understand, recognize, and classify objects in the environment and the world around us

DIRECTIONS

Early Childhood Multiple Intelligences Inventory

Students are to be shown a pair of pictures. The students will be asked to choose from one of the two pictures shown which most appeals to them. Each series of pictures are shown for five to seven second intervals. The teacher is to mark the students' response on the answer key for the corresponding picture sets. After marking all responses, the teacher is to match the answers for each question to the corresponding multiple intelligences box. The teacher will then total the results of each box, finding the top four dominant intelligences for each student.

Early Childhood Multiple Intelligences Test

Name _____ Date _____

Grade _____ Age _____ Sex M____ F____

Answer Key

	A	B
1	1	2
2	3	4
3	5	6
4	7	8
5	1	3
6	2	4
7	5	7
8	6	8
9	1	4
10	2	7
11	3	6
12	5	8
13	1	5
14	6	4

	A	B
15	3	7
16	2	8
17	1	6
18	2	5
19	3	8
20	4	7
21	1	7
22	2	6
23	3	5
24	4	8
25	1	8
26	2	3
27	4	5
28	6	7

Total								
	1. Verbal	2. Math	3. Visual	4. Body	5. Music	6. People	7. Self	8. Nature

Top Dominant Intelligences

1. _____ 2. _____ 3. _____ 4. _____

A.

Listen to books on tape

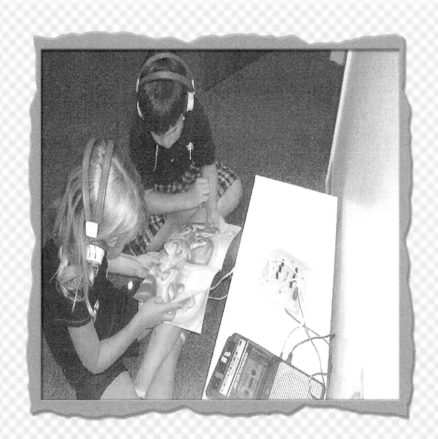

B.

Play with blocks

A.

Use lacing cards

B.

Walk on the balance beam

A.

Listen
to the
C.D. player

B.

Tell stories

A.

Have alone
time

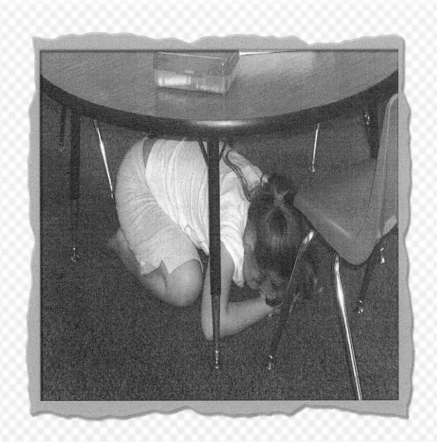

B.

Fill a bird
feeder

A.

Write in a diary

B.

Cut with scissors

A.

Play dominos

B.

Play catch

A.

Play the maracas

B.

Be alone in the reading center

A.

Play
together

B.

Look at the
turtle shell

A.

Write letters

B.

Play bean
bag toss

A.

Use a
balance scale

B.

Have your
own supplies

A.

Use sidewalk
chalk

B.

Play with
a baby

A.

Play the guitar

B.

Smell flowers

A.

Use puppets

B.

Use rhythm
sticks

A.

Play board games

B.

Twirl a baton

A.

Play at the
train table

B.

Use work
mats

A.

Use shapes

B.

Go fishing

A.

Use alphabet
stamps

B.

Work on group
projects

A.

Use a tape
measure

B.

Dance

A.

Make collages

B.

Watch clouds

A.

Go bowling

B.

Write in journals

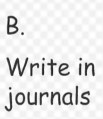

A.

Use play-dough

B.

Make a self
portrait

A.

Use puzzles

B.

Act out stories

A.

Play dress-up

B.

Use cymbals

A.

Climb on the equipment

B.

Work in a garden

A.

Look at
magazines

B.

Use a
bug box

A.

Use a cash register

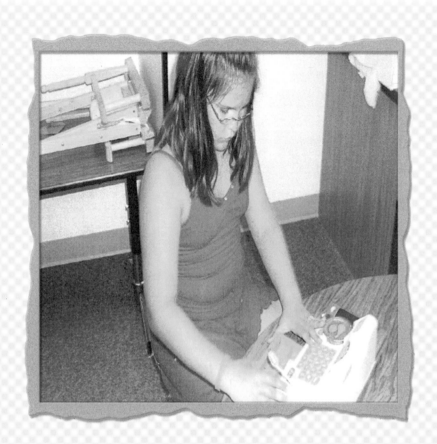

B.

Use color paddles

A.

Play hopscotch

B.

Use a
recorder

A.
Run in a three-
legged race

B.

Use earphones

Lightning Source UK Ltd.
Milton Keynes UK
UKRC020004271118
333029UK00006B/179

9781436364997